THE STORY OF
SLAVERY

Sarah Courtauld

Designed by Karen Tomlins

AM I NOT A MAN & A BROTHER

History consultant: James Walvin
Professor of History, University of York

Edited by Jane Chisholm and Susanna Davidson

First published in 2007 by Usborne Publishing Ltd,
Usborne House, 83-85 Saffron Hill, London EC1N 8RT, England.
www.usborne.com

ACKNOWLEDGEMENTS

(b = bottom, t = top)

Cover © (tl) CORBIS, (tr) Bettmann/CORBIS, (b) Louie Psihoyos/CORBIS, (m) Adam
Woolfitt/CORBIS, back cover © Bridgeman (Bibliotheque de L'Arsenal, Paris, France, Archives
Charmet/The Bridgeman Art Library); **AKG Images** © pp2-3 (akg Images/British Library), pp4-5
(Hervé Champollion/akg-images), p14-15 (akg-images/British Library), p29; **Alamy** © pp6-7 (Chris
Howes/Wild Places Photography/Alamy); **Bridgeman** © p1 (Wilberforce House, Hull City Museums
and Art Galleries, UK/Bridgeman Art Library), p9 (Trustees of the Royal Watercolour Society,
London, UK), pp10-11 (Private Collection, The Stapleton Collection/The Bridgeman Art Library),
p12-13 Private Collection, The Stapleton Collection/The Bridgeman Art Library), p16 (Bibliotheque
de L'Arsenal, Paris, France, Archives Charmet/The Bridgeman Art Library), p20 (Private
Collection/The Bridgeman Art Library), p22 (b) (Wilberforce House, Hull City Museums and Art
Galleries, UK/The Bridgeman Art Library), p23 (t) (Private Collection, Peter Newark American
Pictures/The Bridgeman Art Library), p31 (Private Collection, Peter Newark American
Pictures/The Bridgeman Art Library), p37 (Library of Congress, Washington D.C., USA/The
Bridgeman Art Library), p45 (b) (Biblioteca Nacional, Rio de Janeiro, Brazil/The Bridgeman Art
Library), p49 (b) (British Library Board, All Rights Reserved/The Bridgeman Art Library), p52 (b)
(Wilberforce House, Hull City Museums and Art Galleries, UK/The Bridgeman Art Library), pp54-
55 (b) (Chateau de Versailles, France, Lauros/Giraudon/The Bridgeman Art Library), p59 (Private
Collection/The Bridgeman Art Library), p64 (Brooklyn Museum of Art, New York, USA/The
Bridgeman Art Library); **Camera Press** © p60 (BENOIT GYSEMBERGH, CAMERA PRESS
LONDON); **CORBIS** © pp18-19 (Louie Psihoyos/CORBIS), p21 (Bettmann/CORBIS), p25
(Bettmann/CORBIS), p27 (b) (Bettmann/CORBIS), p32 (Bettmann/CORBIS), p34
(Bettmann/CORBIS), p38 (b) (Bettmann/CORBIS), p39 (t) (Bettmann/CORBIS), p40
(Bettmann/CORBIS), p44 (Hulton-Deutsch Collection/CORBIS), p 61 (ILYAS DEAN/CORBIS
SYGMA); **Getty Images** © pp56-57, p60; **Library of Congress** p20 Prints & Photographs Division,
[LC-USZC4-6204], p24 (William A Stephens), p37 Prints and Photographs Division
[LC-USZ62-76205]; **Mary Evans Picture Library** © p48; **National Maritime Museum** © p46;
Still Pictures © p62; **Tophoto** © p8 (b) (Topham Picturepoint TopFoto.co.uk).

Contents

This 19th century painting shows slaves working on a plantation in Antigua, in the Caribbean.

This Ancient Egyptian wall painting shows a slave anointing his master with oil. Below, another slave is being beaten.

Chapter 1

The first slaves

In ancient times, there were people all over the world who lived without freedom. Forced to work from dawn until dusk, many were fed on scraps of food and treated more like animals than people. They could be bought or sold, just like cattle, and were never paid for their work. If they didn't work hard enough, their masters might beat them.

These people were known as slaves, and their story is one of the ugliest tales in human history.

Many brave slaves tried to escape, but if they were caught, they were severely punished. Some owners even marked their slaves with tattoos, or branding irons, that burned deep into their skin. Then it was almost impossible to escape undetected.

All kinds of people could end up as slaves. Some were forced into slavery as a punishment for a crime. Others sold their own children into slavery when they couldn't afford to take care of them.

Many people became slaves after being captured in wars. In Ancient Egypt, one man described how invading soldiers rushed into his house, grabbed his wife and child, and kidnapped them. "I tried to fight the soldiers, but they attacked me," he wrote. "My family is gone."

Female slaves were mainly forced to do housework, while men were made to do the most physically exhausting jobs. Some of the unluckiest slaves in Ancient Greece worked in mines, digging in tunnels that seeped out poisonous fumes. But there were also skilled slaves in trusted positions who were highly respected. The Ancient Greeks had slaves in their army, while the Ancient Romans had slaves who worked as doctors.

This wall painting shows two slaves at work in a palace in Ancient Greece.

Romans also used slaves for entertainment, by training them to fight each other in front of cheering crowds. These slaves, known as gladiators, often had to fight to the death.

Sometimes masters set their slaves free after years of faithful service. But for the less skilled slaves, freedom was a distant hope. Those who rebelled were punished brutally. One Roman citizen, Vedius Pollio, fed his disobedient slaves to his pet fish.

Some people protested against slavery, but the Romans would never abolish it – it was far too useful to them.

This badge was worn by a Roman slave who had tried to run away. The inscription reads: "Hold me in case I escape."

Chapter 2

Into Africa

During the Middle Ages, slavery continued to exist all over the world. From the 9th century, fierce seafaring warriors from Scandinavia, known as Vikings, sailed all over Europe. When they arrived at the coasts of Britain and Ireland, their attacks were swift and brutal.

They sailed their ships onto beaches, then ran ashore and raided villages, grabbing men and women to sell as slaves. They took their prisoners as far away as Iceland, exchanging them for wine, silks, silver and gold.

From the 13th century, slavery began to fade away in western Europe. New laws were passed, making slaves into serfs. Serfs weren't free citizens – they had to work all their lives for their local lord. But, unlike slaves, they couldn't be bought or sold.

Meanwhile, a new religion, Islam, had spread through the Middle East and North Africa. Its followers, known as Muslims,

Slaves, forced by their captors to cross the Sahara Desert, were often hit by terrifying sand storms.

fought many battles to conquer new lands.

Muslims didn't believe in making slaves of their own people. So they journeyed deep into Africa to find slaves, and marched them back across the scorching Sahara Desert. By the 15th century, thousands of Africans were being kidnapped from their homes each year.

But there was worse to come. The Europeans were about to begin a new slave trade, on a scale never seen before.

This map shows slave routes across the Sahara into the Middle East.

The Middle East

Slave markets

Sahara Desert

Slaves were kidnapped or bought from traders in Central Africa.

Africa

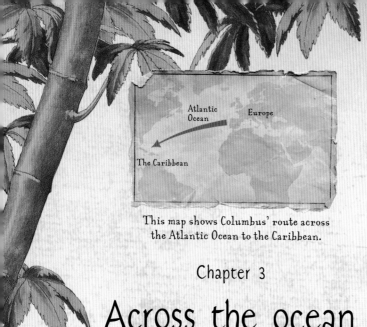

This map shows Columbus' route across
the Atlantic Ocean to the Caribbean.

Chapter 3

Across the ocean

In 1492, an explorer named Christopher
Columbus was sent by the King of Spain to
voyage across the world. Stories had come to
Europe of faraway lands brimming with gold,
and Columbus was determined to find them.

He set sail across the Atlantic, and after
many weeks, he spotted the islands of the
Caribbean. Columbus wrote that the locals
were "gentle people, who lived without killing
or stealing". He founded Spanish settlements

on several of the islands. Soon the Spanish built huge sugar farms there, known as plantations, and forced the local people to work on the farms, as slaves. They were treated brutally, and many died.

Years later, a Spanish monk, Las Casas, visited the plantations, and was horrified by what he saw. He begged the King of Spain to use slaves from Africa, instead of making free men into slaves. He thought it would be fairer, as slavery already existed in some African societies.

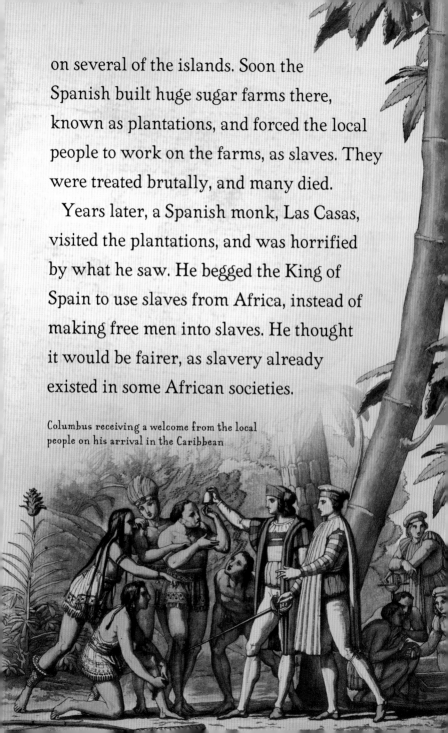

Columbus receiving a welcome from the local people on his arrival in the Caribbean

Soon the Spanish ships arrived from West Africa, crammed full of men and women. They were quickly set to work on the farms, harvesting sugar to send back to Spain. The Spanish treated the Africans cruelly too. Many died, but the Spanish simply shipped in more to replace them.

In Europe, people loved pastries and sweet drinks, and paid high prices for Caribbean sugar. Over the next hundred years, the plantations in the Caribbean had made slave owners and traders very rich.

Soon other European countries rushed to conquer land across the Atlantic Ocean. Like the Spanish before them, they brought slaves from Africa to work on their plantations, farming sugar, tobacco and coffee.

In total, more than 11 million Africans were carried across the sea to a life of slavery. It became one of the most brutal episodes in human history.

This 19th century painting shows men, women and children at work on a sugar plantation in Antigua, in the Caribbean.

On long journeys, slaves were chained together like this.

Chapter 4

A slave's journey

The route from Europe to West Africa, and on to America and the Caribbean, became known as the slave triangle. During the 18th century, thousands of ships set out to make the journey each year, from European ports such as Liverpool, Lisbon and Seville.

One of the slaves was a boy named Ottobah Cugoano, who later wrote down his story. He was barely twelve years old when raiders kidnapped him from his West African village. Ottobah had been playing in the woods with his friends, when suddenly he was grabbed from behind and thrown over someone's shoulder. His captors pelted away through the trees. When they came to a stop, Ottobah was thrown down onto the dirt. He looked up to see two huge men standing over him.

This map shows the route slave traders took from Europe to Africa, across to the Caribbean, and back to Europe. It was known as the slave triangle.

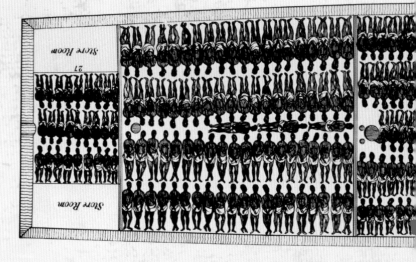

This plan, made by a slave trader, shows how tightly slaves were packed into the hold of a slave ship. Each slave had only the space of a coffin to lie in.

One was holding his friend roughly by his hair, the other pointed a glinting sword at Ottobah's neck. The men quicky bound the children's hands and marched them through the forest. They walked for months until, finally, they reached the sea. The children were separated, and Ottobah was locked in a filthy dungeon. He lay in the dark for days.

One morning, a strange, pale man marched

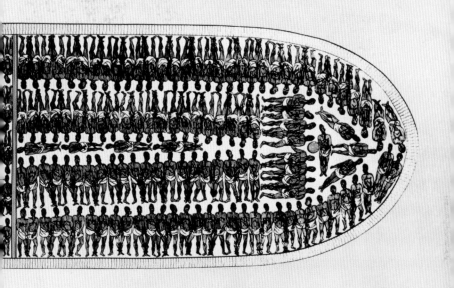

him out of the cell and down to the waterfront.
Within minutes he was forced onto the deck of
a large wooden ship, before being shoved into
the stinking hold where hundreds of people
were packed tightly together in the dark.

As the ship sailed out to sea, the prisoners
crashed against each other with every wave.
Soon the floor was covered in a layer of sweat,
urine and blood. One in ten prisoners would
not survive the journey.

An artist named George Cruikshank made this print, which
shows a slave ship captain punishing a female slave.

Some people leaped to freedom – by slipping
past the guards and plunging into the icy
Atlantic Ocean. They would rather die than
go on living as prisoners. Others plotted to
overthrow the slave ship captains. But most
were stopped and cruelly punished.

Chapter 5

Plantation life

After a hellish journey, the slaves arrived on the other side of the ocean. As soon as they left the ship, they were stripped, cleaned and covered in palm oil to make them look healthier. Crowds of curious buyers swarmed around them, prodding them as if they were animals in a market.

Buyers look on as a slave ship arrives, and the slaves are rowed to the shore.

Then the auction began. As each slave stepped up to the stand, the rest of his life could be decided in a few moments.

Auctions were often the scenes of sad farewells. In 1851, a bystander described a slave auction in St. Louis, in the United States. When a young man was sold, he rushed to his new master and begged him to buy his wife too.

"I don't want her," the man snapped. "But I'll take her if she goes cheap."

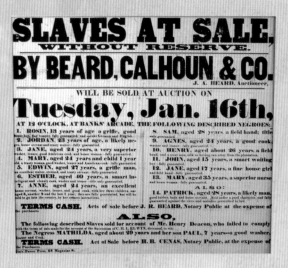

This poster advertises a slave auction in the United States.

This 19th century painting shows a slave auction in Virginia, in the United States.

As his new owner bid, the young man's face lit up. But when another man offered a higher price for his wife, tears rolled down his cheeks. Soon, the woman was sold – but not to her husband's master.

The young man ran to his wife. "We are to part on earth," he said. "I hope you'll try to meet me in heaven. I'll try to meet you there."

In this painting, a female slave begs the slave owner who has bought her husband to buy her and her baby as well.

Most slaves were taken to plantations, where they were routinely whipped and beaten. Slaves who worked in people's homes had an easier life. But they lived under the watchful eyes of their masters. If they misbehaved, they could expect to have an ear cut off, be flogged or even killed.

Life was hardest for those who worked in the Caribbean and in South America. There, some plantation owners invented horrifying punishments for rebel slaves, such as burying them alive.

Meanwhile, in Europe, scientists and thinkers were developing theories that Africans were inferior to other people. These racist ideas quickly became popular, making slavery seem more acceptable.

While plantation owners treated the Africans as if they were stupid, many slaves used this to their advantage. Some let farm animals loose, ruined their owners' clothes, smashed up the best dinner plates – and then pretended it was all an accident.

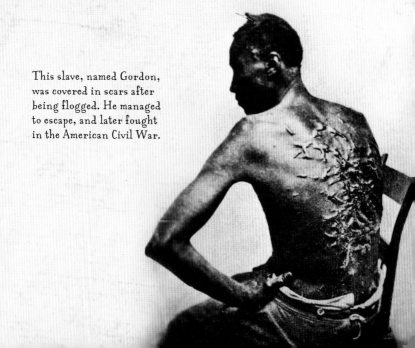

This slave, named Gordon, was covered in scars after being flogged. He managed to escape, and later fought in the American Civil War.

When slaves stopped acting dumb, their owners got a shock. There is a well-known story of a Jamaican slave named Pompey who got the better of his master. One day, his owner was standing in front of the mirror in his bedroom, admiring his new outfit.

"Pompey, how do I look?" he asked.

"Why, sir, you look mighty – just like a lion," Pompey replied.

"Why, Pompey, where have you ever seen a lion?" the master asked.

"I saw one down in yonder field the other day, massa," Pompey replied.

"Pompey, you foolish fellow, that was a jackass," said the master, smiling.

"Was it, sir?" Pompey replied. "Well, sir, you look just like him."

Slaves had hard, painful lives, but they weren't miserable all the time. On public holidays, they were allowed to dance.

They played banjos, violins and home-made instruments, and danced and sang together. Slaves also sang as they worked in the fields, and they poured all the heartbreak of their lives into haunting, soaring melodies.

"I see star-rise, I see moon-rise,
I'll lie in my grave and stretch out my arms,
And my soul and thy soul will meet that day,
When I lay my body down."

A group of slaves listen to a man singing and playing the banjo.

Many plantation slaves sang religious songs. But these songs were often loaded with secret meanings.

> *"A band of angels comin' after me,*
> *Comin' for to carry me home,"*

went the words of one famous slave song. The plantation owners assumed the slaves were singing about heaven, but they were secretly singing about what they all hoped for on earth – someone who would help them to escape.

Some slaves got the chance to buy their freedom from their owners. One man named Olaudah Equiano, who worked on a ship in the Caribbean, was promised his freedom by his owner, in return for forty pounds. Olaudah earned money by trading goods from island to island. After a year's hard work, he raised the money, and took it to his owner, Robert King.

"I'd never have said forty pounds if I

thought you'd get it so soon," scowled Robert. But the captain of the ship was furious with him. "You should never break a promise," he said angrily. Eventually, Robert gave in.

As Olaudah stepped off the ship, he was sure there was no one on earth as happy as he was. "I'm free!" he shouted to everyone he met. "This is the best day of my life!" He ran like lightning through the streets, his feet hardly touching the ground.

Many slaves were able to earn some money for themselves, but few ever raised enough to buy their freedom, as Olaudah had done. So, their best chance was to run away.

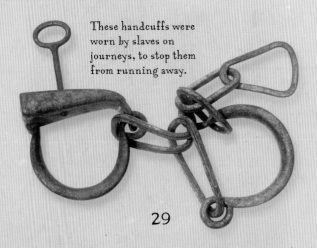

These handcuffs were worn by slaves on journeys, to stop them from running away.

Chapter 6

Great escapes

Fearless and inventive, many slaves dreamed up astonishing ways of escaping their masters and finding their loved ones. They wore disguises, stowed away on ships, and sped hundreds of miles on top of train roofs, clinging on for their lives.

Some of the most ingenious escape stories come from the United States. By the 19th century, slavery had been abolished in many of the northern states, but still existed in the southern states. So, many slaves tried to escape to the north, even though slave catchers scoured the roads, and plantation owners sent packs of vicious hounds after them.

In this engraving, a slave catcher chases an escaping slave with a pack of hounds.

CAUTION!!
COLORED PEOPLE
OF BOSTON, ONE & ALL,
You are hereby respectfully CAUTIONED and advised, to avoid conversing with the
Watchmen and Police Officers of Boston,
For since the recent ORDER OF THE MAYOR & ALDERMEN, they are empowered to act as
KIDNAPPERS
AND
Slave Catchers,
And they have already been actually employed in KIDNAPPING, CATCHING, AND KEEPING SLAVES. Therefore, if you value your LIBERTY, and the *Welfare of the Fugitives* among you, *Shun* them in every possible manner, as so many *HOUNDS* on the track of the most unfortunate of your race.

Keep a Sharp Look Out for KIDNAPPERS, and have TOP EYE open.
APRIL 24, 1851.

THEODORE PARKER'S PLACARD
Placard written by Theodore Parker and printed and posted by the Vigilance Committee of Boston after the rendition of Thomas Sims to slavery in April, 1851

This poster warns black people in Boston to look out for kidnappers and slave catchers.

One runaway was a courageous man named Henry Brown. While he was working in the fields one morning, he was told that his wife and son had been sold to a new owner.

That night, Henry wept. His owner had promised he would never split up Henry's family. Now he knew if he stayed on the plantation, he would never see them again. So he decided to run away.

He had heard of a famous anti-slavery campaigner, named James McKim, who lived in Philadelphia, in the north. If he could get to McKim, he knew he would help him. It seemed like an impossible task. But then a brilliant idea flashed through his mind.

With the help of a friend, Henry hid himself inside a large, wooden box. He sent a message ahead to McKim, and then had himself sent to McKim's house in Philadelphia.

For three days, Henry lay in total darkness, terrified that at any moment the box would break, and he would be discovered. He had written, "This side up with care" on it, but no one paid any attention. So he spent several miles on his head.

Finally, the box was delivered to James McKim's house, where a group of men were waiting anxiously.

"Is it alright inside?" James shouted, rapping loudly on the lid of the box. There was a deathly silence.

Then, from inside, came a trembling voice. "Yes, yes, I'm alright," whispered Henry. Quickly, the men opened up the box, clapping as Henry staggered out – and fainted to the floor.

After his escape, Henry became known as "Henry Box Brown".

Henry never found his family, but he spent the rest of his life helping runaways. He worked with James McKim on the Underground Railroad, a secret network which helped slaves escape to the free states in the north.

The Railroad was made up of houses, called stations, run by station masters, that offered food and shelter to slaves on the run. It had been started in 1787 by a Quaker, Isaac Hopper. The Quakers were a group of radical Christians, who believed slavery was wrong.

After they had given the runaways a bed for the night, the station masters bundled them into the backs of wagons, to take them to the next station on the route. Most slaves hid under piles of cloth, but some wagons had secret compartments for them to hide in. When the wagons were searched, the runaways lay absolutely still, terrified that a single cough or sneeze might give them away. But many were lucky. By 1850, more than 10,000 slaves had used the Underground Railroad to escape.

In 1851, a young slave from Maryland, named Harriet Tubman, heard about the Underground Railroad, and decided to try to escape. At midnight, she and her brothers slipped out of their quarters.

But, before long, Harriet's brothers begged her to turn back. They were terrified of being caught. Harriet hugged them tight, and sadly watched them walk away until they were out of sight.

Now she was all alone. "I have a right to two things," she said to herself, "liberty, or death. If I can't have one, I'll have the other. But I'll fight for liberty as long as I have the strength."

On her long journey north, Harriet slept under the stars, and ate whatever she could find. But sometimes, in the middle of the night, she would come across a house with a candle shining brightly in the window. Then she knew that the house was a station on the Underground Railroad, and she would be welcome there.

Harriet eventually reached the north, but it wasn't long before she raised enough money to go back south, to rescue other slaves. She went

This engraving, made in 1872, shows a fight breaking out, as slave catchers discover runaway slaves inside a wagon.

to plantations in secret, to meet groups of trembling people gathered at chosen hiding places, secretly waiting for her to guide them to freedom.

Harriet made 19 trips on the Underground Railroad, and helped more than 300 people to escape. She led the runaways over rocky mountains, through icy streams and dense forests. Sometimes, with bleeding feet, the exhausted slaves were ready to give up.

On one journey, an old and terrified slave knelt before her, begging her to let him return to the plantation. Harriet pulled out a gun, pointed it at his head and bellowed at him: "Dead men tell no tales – go on or die!"

Harriet soon became so famous, the slave owners offered a reward for her capture. She lived in constant danger of being arrested. One day, she fell asleep in a train station under her own "Wanted" poster. When she woke up, two men were reading the poster aloud. "Wanted: Harriet Tubman. Illiterate, dangerous runaway slave. Reward: $40,000."

Harriet Tubman with her rifle

Harriet Tubman, on the far left, with a
group of ex-slaves she had helped to free

"That's her!" cried one of the men, looking
straight at Harriet. But she calmly picked up a
book that was lying on the floor, and
pretended to read. It was enough to fool them.
The two men walked away.

Many people risked their lives taking slaves
to safety. The slave masters hated runaways
and all who helped them. But there was one
thing that terrified them more than anything
else: a slave revolt.

An 18th century painting showing Leonard Parkinson, a Jamaican slave leader who fought against the British.

Chapter 7

Uprising!

Throughout history, hundreds of courageous slaves have fought against their masters. One of the most famous was a Roman slave named Spartacus, who led an uprising against the Roman army over 2,000 years ago. For three years, he won battle after battle, until a Roman general named Crassus defeated him. Spartacus was killed in battle, and 6,000 of his followers were crucified.

But not all slave revolts ended in tragedy. In 1789, the Caribbean island of Haiti was a French settlement, where thousands of people slaved away on sugar plantations.

One of the slaves was a quiet, solitary man named Toussaint L'Ouverture. His master was very lenient: he never struck Toussaint and let him learn to read and write. There was a passage in one book that Toussaint read over and over again:

Everyone has a right to liberty. A courageous chief is needed to give the slaves their freedom. Where is this courageous man? He will appear, and everyone will praise him.

As he read those words, Toussaint had no doubt that he would be that leader.

Toussaint L'Ouverture, from a 19th century print

The book had been written by a Frenchman named Abbé Raynal, who believed everyone had a right to be free. He was one of a group of rebellious thinkers whose ideas about equality were spreading through France.

In 1789, the rebels led an uprising, and revolution gripped Paris. The king was executed, and France became a republic. The revolutionaries inspired the slaves in Haiti to revolt. Within four years, Toussaint governed the island, and slavery was banned.

This 18th century print shows riots breaking out in Haiti, and slave owners fleeing.

Then, a new French leader, Napoloeon, tried to invade Haiti to bring back slavery. Although Napoleon was the greatest general of the time, Toussaint's army managed to hold out against him. But when Toussaint met Napoleon to make peace, he was tricked and taken back to France in chains.

Just two years later, Napoleon was defeated, and Haiti became independent. The victory sent tremors of excitement through slave settlements – and waves of fear across Europe.

This print, by cartoonist James Gillray, shows the grotesque side of luxurious lifestyles in 18th century England.

Chapter 8

Breaking the chains

In the 18th century, London was a busy, prosperous city. Bakeries were crammed with twenty different types of cake, from sponges to gingerbread. Bustling coffee houses opened all day and half the night, and men smoked tobacco and took snuff. The nation was hooked on chocolate, and a sweet cup of tea was quickly becoming a national addiction.

No one mentioned the invisible ingredient in all these goods: slavery. The slave trade was at the heart of London's wealth, and for many years, even the Church of England and the royal family had been closely involved. The Duke of York, later King James II, had ordered his initials to be stamped on the 3,000 African slaves he owned.

Slave trading was a respectable profession. But by the 1760s, many people were becoming horrified by tales of violent slave masters.

Many artists painted images like this one to show people how cruel slave punishments were.

On a cold and rainy night in 1765, a young man named Jonathan Strong staggered into a house in Mincing Lane, London, looking desperately for the doctor who lived there. He was covered in blood, and he could hardly see.

The doctor, William Sharp, and his brother Granville, rushed the man to a hospital, where he told them his story. Jonathan Strong was a slave, and his master had attacked him with a pistol.

Granville visited Jonathan over the next few months. Once he had recovered, they said their farewells.

Two years later, a letter arrived.

Granville Sharp with Jonathan Strong

Dear Granville,

My old master found me and kidnapped me. He locked me in prison, and he's going to send me to Jamaica.

Please help,
Jonathan Strong

Granville rushed to the prison and begged the warden to let Jonathan go. He refused. Soon the case was in the courts. Granville knew nothing about the law, but he studied hard and fought for Jonathan's freedom.

One hot June morning, the judge read out the sentence. "You are free to go," he said. Jonathan sat in stunned silence, too happy to say a word.

Granville quickly became known as a friend of slaves. He led a group calling themselves abolitionists, who campaigned to end the trade.

Ignatius Sancho had his portrait painted by a famous artist of the day, Thomas Gainsborough.

Another famous abolitionist was a man named Ignatius Sancho. He had been born on a slave ship, and brought to London as a child slave. After he had bought his freedom, he lived in Westminster, where he composed music, and kept a grocery shop. Sancho wrote hundreds of letters to his friends, begging them to do all they could to stop the slave trade.

When Sancho died in 1780, his letters were published, and became an overnight sensation. Slave owners liked to claim that Africans were uncivilized and stupid, so it was fair to treat them like animals. But Sancho's letters showed that he was witty, intelligent and kind.

Then, in 1789, a freed slave named Olaudah Equiano published the story of his life. After winning his freedom, he had been the first African explorer in the Arctic. Thousands of people rushed to buy the tale of his life as a slave, and his adventures as a free man.

It was becoming obvious to many people in Britain that there were people in the world who were brutal, cruel and uncivilized. But they weren't the Africans. They were the men who made them slaves.

This is the first page from Olaudah Equiano's bestselling book, which helped persuade people that the slave trade should be abolished.

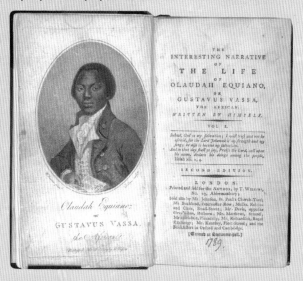

One night, Olaudah visited Granville Sharp with news of a shocking new case. A slave captain, Luke Collingwood, was sailing on the *Zong*, a ship taking slaves to Jamaica. During the journey, many of the slaves became sick. Collingwood knew that if they died, the owners of the *Zong* would lose all their money.

So he killed 130 of the slaves, by tossing them into the Atlantic Ocean. He hoped that the *Zong's* owners might be able to claim insurance money for each dead man.

Soon the case ended up in the law courts. Granville watched, horrified, as the *Zong's* lawyer rose to address the crowd.

This engraving, made in 1822, shows a slave captain throwing slaves overboard.

"All this talk of murder is nonsense," he declared calmly. "This is a mere case of goods."

It sounded shocking, but it was true. In English law, slaves weren't even classed as human beings.

The case spurred the abolitionists into action. In 1787, Granville and his friend Thomas Clarkson founded the *Society for the Abolition of the Slave Trade.* They published articles in newspapers, and gathered evidence to convince people how cruel the slave trade really was.

The abolitionists met with fierce opposition, as many people believed that Britain's wealth depended on the slave trade. But a famous philosopher, Adam Smith, claimed the opposite – that ending the slave trade would actually create more money. As his views spread, more and more people accepted that it was time for the trade to end.

While Granville Sharp was defending slaves in court, and Thomas Clarkson was looking for evidence, a politician, William Wilberforce, was fighting in parliament.

In 1789, he gave his first speech on slavery in the House of Commons. He spoke for three hours on the horrors of the slave trade, and caused a sensation.

William Wilberforce's dramatic speeches won him the title "the nightingale of the Commons".

By the end, his voice thundered across the room. "Having heard all this, you may turn the other way, but you can never again say that you did not know."

Wilberforce's speeches were impressive, but the slave owners were very powerful in parliament. Every year, for the next nine years, Wilberforce introduced a new bill against the slave trade. Each one was defeated.

Finally, on the February 23, 1807, Wilberforce's latest motion to end the slave trade was debated in the House of Commons. One by one, politicians rose and spoke, each in support of abolition. Wilberforce put his head in his hands and wept with joy. For more than thirty years, thousands of people had campaigned to end the slave trade. Finally, they were going to win.

The vote was passed by 283 to 16, and the British slave trade was abolished. No more

British ships would be allowed to take slaves across the Atlantic. Celebrations broke out on plantations everywhere. But the abolitionists soon realized that stopping the trade wasn't enough. People could no longer buy or sell slaves, but they could still own them. The abolitionists had to end slavery itself.

This French painting shows celebrations in 1848, when slavery was abolished in French colonies.

So, for twenty years, they campaigned tirelessly. In 1833, slavery was abolished throughout the British Empire.

The British government paid £20 million as compensation to the plantation owners, but the slaves themselves received no compensation at all.

Chapter 9

Slaves at war

Meanwhile, in the south of the United States, slavery was still flourishing. During the 1850s, runaways such as Frederick Douglass urged slaves to revolt. "You have seen how a man becomes a slave," he wrote, "now you shall see how a slave becomes a man."

Sojourner Truth was another escaped slave, who made passionate speeches against slavery.

After one of her speeches, a man turned to her with disdain. "Miss Truth, your speeches are worth nothing more than a fleabite," he said.

"Maybe not, but God willing, I'll keep you scratching," she snapped back.

Still, no matter how hard the campaigners worked, the southern states stubbornly defended slavery. It was just one of many issues that divided North and South. Soon, tensions rose to boiling point, and in 1861 they exploded – into a bloody civil war.

This re-enactment of a scene from the American Civil War shows what a battlefield would have looked like.

After two years of fighting, the leader of the northern states, Abraham Lincoln, invited black men to join his army, to defeat the South, and slavery, for good. More than 190,000 black soldiers fought on the northern side.

In 1865, the South was defeated, and slavery was finally abolished all over the United States. For two hundred years, the slaves had dreamed of a single goal – liberty. At last, they were free. On plantations, people were dumbfounded. Their lives had changed forever, in the course of a single day.

This photograph shows a brother and sister, ex-slaves who were rescued from the South by a soldier in the American Civil War.

These ex-slaves were rescued from a slave ship by the British Navy in 1890.

Chapter 10

The end of slavery?

B y 1900, the slave trade no longer officially existed, but in many parts of the world it carried on – illegally. Slave traders were still using the old routes across the Sahara Desert to slave markets in the Middle East. From there, slaves were sold on, and some were taken as far away as India.

During the 20th century, many countries worked together to try to stamp out slavery. But they didn't succeed.

A child slave working in a mine in Colombia in the 1980s

Today slavery still goes on all over the world. In India and Pakistan, millions of workers are forced to work for whole lifetimes to pay off debts. In Eastern Europe, slave gangs trick women into coming to richer countries such as the United Kingdom. When they arrive, the gangs lock them up, and make them work for nothing.

In a small town called Sikasso, in Mali, West Africa, police files record hundreds of missing children. Slave traders kidnap them and force them to work on chocolate plantations in the nearby Ivory Coast.

These are some of many examples of modern slavery. There are more than 12.5 million slaves in the world today, and slave traders still make huge fortunes out of human misery. Nowadays the trade is known as human trafficking, and is worth thousands of millions of dollars each year.

But slavery faces more opposition than ever before. All over the world, thousands of people are working to combat it.

Young people protest against child slavery in Pakistan.

One civil rights worker, John Eibner, has gone undercover on 20 journeys across Sudan, where more than 15,000 people have been forced into slavery, including many children. Eibner buys slaves from their owners, and then helps them return to their homes.

There are many more people like him, working all over the world to combat slavery in different ways. Slavery has not ended, but there are more people fighting it now than ever before.

Ex-slaves returning to their homeland after being freed

SLAVERY TIMELINE

1750BC The very first laws are written down. These include rules for the punishment of slaves.

1000BC Slavery exists all over the globe, from China to Egypt.

73BC Spartacus leads a slave revolt against the Romans.

800 Around this time, the East African slave trade begins, taking slaves from Africa to the Middle East.

1502 The first African slaves are taken to the Caribbean.

1787 Society for the Abolition of the Slave Trade founded in London.

1789 The French Revolution proclaims the ideals of "equality and liberty" for all.

1791 Slaves lead an uprising in Haiti.

1804 Haiti becomes an independent republic.

1807 The slave trade is abolished in Britain.

1833 Slavery is abolished in British colonies.

1841 Britain, France, Russia, Prussia and Austria agree to stop the slave trade on the seas.

1865 Slavery is abolished in the United States.

1873 The slave market in Zanzibar, one of the busiest in East Africa, is closed.

1888 Slavery is abolished in Brazil.

1936 Slavery is made illegal in Northern Nigeria.

1949 The United Nations holds a convention against human trafficking.

2005 The UN estimates that 1.2 million children are trafficked each year.

A note on dates: some early dates are written as "BC", which stands for "Before Christ". BC dates are counted back from the year 1, the traditional date for the birth of Jesus Christ. The bigger a number, the longer ago the date.

INDEX

Internet Links

For links to websites where you can find out more
about slavery go to the Usborne Quicklinks Website at
www.usborne-quicklinks.com and type the keywords **YR Slavery**.
The recommended websites are regularly reviewed and updated
but, please note, Usborne Publishing is not responsible for
the content of websites other than its own.

An American 19th
century painting
showing slaves
escaping